GETTING READY FOR A DATE

GETTING READY FOR A DATE

poems by

Peter Wild

GHOST PONY PRESS

Printed in the United States of America
First Edition

ISBN: 0-941160-09-2

Some of the following poems previously appeared in Abraxas, American Poetry Review, Angelstone, Black Warrior Review, Chariton Review, Columbia, Goblets, Gramercy Review, Images, Memphis State Review, Michigan Quarterly Review, New Mexico Humanities Review, Northwest Review, Prairie Schooner, Quarterly West, and Vegetable Box.

GHOST PONY PRESS
2518 Gregory Street
Madison, Wisconsin
53711

for Rosemary

¿Qué tienes en tus manos
de primavera?

CONTENTS

A special signed edition limited to 150 copies

CLIMBERS

Already I'm falling back
into my old habits,
standing around in my railroad cap,
slumped beside you in the back of the Jeep
with a comfortable globe of tobacco in my mouth.
You jab me with your finger: "People
will say we're in love," you shout
as we take a bounce, and waking near the roof
I begin throwing stones at the cows
who all the way in dash off like horses,
deer, chickens in a barnyard
invaded by Huns. At the saddle
                    we let the others attack the rock,
groaning up on their skeins of rope, while bushed
from last night we sprawl where they hid bearing
their water up full of fear
in this nook among boulders watching
up and down the long valley for
things to move. You keep turning
                the yellow splinters of your eyes on me
while I make circles, boxes, labyrinths in the sand
with what is left of their broken pots, knowing
that once inside you I will never get out.
But in an hour we start as they halloo,
                                their voices raying
from the little burnt figures at the top,
the gods of the mountain waving down at us.

FARM

In the morning, still without their provender
the soldiers sit by the side of the road
nursing the broken clavicles they got
last night when they dreamt
they were working on a farm and
                that Great Farmer the sun
stood grinning in the loft throwing down
sacks of grain to them, a hideous banker
proving the worth of his own bank.

Now feeling sorry for themselves
they begin to whirl and dance,
singing through their nasal passages
like violated choirboys afraid to go home,
dervishes so treasuring their new trance
they'll never play the violin again.

But down the hill someone is calling out
from the door of a blasted farmhouse, wild laundrywoman
as stern and confident as Barbara Frietchie
who just yesterday solved the problem of her life
by sending her hydrophobic daughter galloping out
to chase the redcoats down the road on all fours.

She needs a little help,
is willing to pay them well
in cider and apples. And so
remembering their schoolteachers some of them
pause, go, beckoned slowly in
like lost dogs to the front porch
and sets them to work wrenching the long row
of fence posts from the ground
that a carpenter thinking of the Mona Lisa
put in slipshod years ago.

                                "A worker should be
worthy of his hire," she grumbles behind them
as when each takes hold, pulls,
he stands fatidic at the stump in his arms
dripping honey, the curious, prolonged
music of a beehive, a diseased tooth,
the interest rate of phosphorus plucked from water
as each is yanked out.

CHRISTIAN SCIENTISTS

Early on we learned what liberty meant
                                        conducted by a wand
reciting the battles of the Revolution
and in turn dreaming out loud what we'd do with it,
becoming train engineers, farmers,
                              and I the windows in a bus.
But she, squinting, refused to be free,
time after time standing to choke,
her finger on the text but looking toward heaven,
a martyr ready to go up, but sinking at last
back into the snickering sea of the rest of us.
Our daily exemplum: the horse
                    who wouldn't drink, who proved it
always swinging wildly to miss,
                                  and once went down
to break her wrist, keep the red lump
as a relic, and that impressed us.
                                        When the bees got her
and she collapsed, most ran,
but I stood among those stooping
over the exhibition,
                    to be doubly astounded, almost converted
when as her throat closed up
she whispered for her prayer book
then slowly came back to life again,
shaking off the oxygen. That night one uncle
said the sheriff should arrest them for neglect
while another stomping out declared they had more guts
than the whole lot of us. Later lying awake
I heard about her beautiful aunt who years ago
riddled by cancer wheeled herself
to the bridge and eyes closed tight
                                    managed to jump off,
to emerge on the other side
of whatever lay beyond the constant
danger of the mill pond where we swam,
                                  now truly careless in her knowledge
like the Indians we threw popcorn at,
                    proud that no bullets could touch them.

DUCK GIRL

In the woods there is only one sound
I want to hear, their riant voices through the trees,
the nonsense of jewels talking that makes
                    sense only to them discovering themselves all day
as they turn over leaves looking for frogs.
That is the sound of your heart.

And so there you are just as my heart predicted,
a heaven full of cows, what all the indestructible miners
I've known stop to dream of exhausted on their knees underground,
a fierce sun above always going through the trees,
but moving here on earth, soft as the knowledge in a book.
Without a word we stoop, cut the wild rhubarb
leaves from the bank that corrode the mouths
of foundlings, of salesmen lost in the woods and desperate at dark,
becoming the light in their heads that plagues them all night long;
but they come running up to be fed,
then go off back to their bushes whispering "incipit, incipit."

GETTING READY FOR A DATE

There are bad people in every culture.
One learns this from visiting museums.
That's why it's best to live on one's own street
where the trees are familiar brides
and the dogs nod padding off to their business.

But even here, in one's own home,
at night lying awake reviewing your education,
how things have come together, there are other elements,
the shadow of a branch on a window,
some foreign student thrown out, turned robber
standing there for hours filamentous, internalizing
a movie he saw about samurai

Raging across their world. In their cage
the birds are jumping up and down, pointing,
trying to give warning, characters out of Walt Disney,
while up on the closet shelf your wrinkled plastic kite,
the one that almost won the competition,
rolls back and forth, a man with hemorrhoids,
a haughty Florentine painter looking for his brush
                                        or getting ready for a date.

You get up and wander around the country of the kitchen
as if eating a dish of cold spaghetti would make up
for having forgotten to eat the right things all week.
Then at last bowing to lock the front door also remember
the lawn mower sitting stiffly out on the lawn,
a lost hound, alert visitor longing to be invited in,
                                        the mail not yet picked up,
the jeweled keys, music hanging in the truck's ignition.

PRISONERS

When the cat ran into your wife,
                                        scared of being eaten,
she ran out to see it, the droppings
of the lank horse that wanders here she thought
come alive under the creosote bush.
You refused to kill it with the shovel
she'd stationed by the door, hearing the tales,
but instead leaned over, white hands on knees
delighted as it twirled, defining its colors,
your fear in the sunlight. Here
the mail truck passes a mile away, a near visitor,
all night there are no lights from a city,
                                                        only the glow
from the prison far over the horizon,
the blotch after dinner that keeps your lives garish.
Raised on movies, she's afraid of escapes,
robberies, worse . . . and lies awake
hearing them, the thumping in the pooled
                                             shadows that precedes
the moon, yet another false dawn for her about to explode
the top off a lava peak, then testing the barbed wire;
the skunks that make love all night under the kitchen,
or the coyotes, boyfriends from another life
you kid her, waking in her grip,
that sometimes pad up to look in the window,
that you, having learned to sleep,
        to dream of all this, get up to shoo away
with light applause and a whisper.

LAWN MOWERS

In this neighborhood
people are asleep by ten o'clock,
seeking their reward in the sheets,
behind their rows of somber palms,
the unionized guard of a king's court,
or perhaps dreaming of me, more of an athlete,
having sweated earnestly through the day
                                        in bed by nine,
to leap up an hour early and unlike them
perhaps catch a glimpse of the chubby paperboy
flogging himself one-handed
                    as one-handed he weaves on his bicycle
from door to door, of the dogs
who have lain out there, one to each shabby
                back yard, through the interminable hours,
among the doll houses peeling apart,
                    the alert but abandoned lawn mowers,
one steady eye open to what might happen to the world,
wells filling up with themselves, like the ice-cream vendor
looking out from the window of his truck,
who has stayed open all night long
without a customer
  and at last wearily closes the shutter on the morning.

MAKING UP

Because we're fighting again
you detail me to guide the tail,
making sure nobody's lost
from the crowd. After the strict parents,
the long marriage, your life's a wreck,
you've got a lot of time to make up you shout back
rushing to the lead through the oaks
past the astounded city folk, jaws
drooping over their boots. Well then make it
more of a wreck I shout up the trail
remembering the lies. This is
at best a sergeant's honor,
chomping my bit not with you all day
            back here in the dust where it's slow.
And if I had my way, like my old sergeant
in the Army I'd give them what
would bring out their best,
                        delight them the most, one
prolonged dose of discipline to
push them full of fear, eyes bulging up the trail
using a whip, throwing stones until
they fell down at the top full of praise for themselves.
But instead though I'm a barrel of snakes
writhing in tobacco juice, I'm my old kind self.
For hours I suffer the retired bacteriologist
from Chicago who pants in the switchbacks
that at 79, unwed, she's determined to see the world.
Beneath the dizzy peaks I make up the names of flowers
for the mailman from New York, busy all day with my knife
repair blisters, cut off the foot of a crying girl
and with my touch give it back to her, a whole loaf.

But counting bodies after lunch
as you send the chain staggering down notice
two kids have flickered off, full of sarcasm
sing out "Chief Guide, Chief Guide" through my nose,
then plunge into the bushes looking for
their clothes, their fingerprints on trunks. I'm no
St. Christopher, more a cursed Smoky the Bear
aflame with fear, but after hours breaking through alders,

listening for birds, come plunging back
with them on my shoulders. In that way
we spend those last few hours
with them swinging on our hands alone going out,
and telling them stories, singing all the way
                                        down toward the sunset ahead,
     a wounded bear taking his great slice
                              of watermelon with him through the trees,
love, beneath your green hat you keep turning the crushed rock
of your eyes on me while they bounce between us,
and for that one prolonged moment in the dusk
        that wounds like nothing else
  just this once as we walk in our flesh
          we are young, they are ours, ours.

SENDING YOU FLOWERS AT THE MONTESSORI SCHOOL

There you are laboring
in the basement of the Saguaro Christian Church
making a living among other people's children
who bite at your heels
or crammed with imagination
want to be, not bus drivers,
but the windows in a bus.
One, to stay alive, kisses you
on the cheek each morning.
When he comes, a desperate man,
a telephone pole escaping with his box across the landscape,
calling your name in the midst of all this,
everything stops. Because I was raised like this
        the message says in Spanish
"What signs of Spring do you carry in your hands?"
which shoot up, for a moment
                        flutter around your face
like the sausages the butcher's wife in the story
holds up from the dogs dancing around her
before they settle down, and you explain.

FREE CLIMBING

In the middle of the week
we can't go far, but far enough
with these few hours to sit
here on the edge of our lives
                    idly eating carrots
as around us the towheaded cactus forest
spurts out of its lava pyre.
Below us the city verges, digs in its claws.
And finally following the siren
floating through the canyon, we spot it
speeding slowly up Gates Pass
then down around the plugs,
                    racing out on the flats
to pick up the sticks we can
barely see, over there near the
Desert Museum, where two cars have become one.
You sit in your straw hat, the shape
of a wave you bought in California,
                    too small for the longer stretches,
but just right for the tight places,
                    doing leg jams, fist slams,
then going through your slow paces flat against the backdrop
                    of a cliff,
face concentrated, like a saint coming to make some announcement
from the corner of a medieval painting.
We turn to face the rock again, touching it
with our lips all the way for the final pitch.
In the lead, you disappear into the sharp shadow of a chimney
as I follow step by step behind to be safe,
resting, testing it, then pulling ourselves up over
                    the rotten musky rock
that keeps raining, pulling away around us,
toward the little flap of sky overhead.

CAMOUFLAGE

When we crouch in the mesquite grove
watching for birds, there is the head,
the neatly bearded face of John Steinbeck
worried about his hemorrhoids
floating out of the fleshy dawn
toward us over the thorns. It is the oracle
that has followed us in the pre-morning,
a one-man choir chanting in Latin, answering himself.
                    In this canyon I rise for small talk
but he says at once he's lonely,
                        an immigrant from Switzerland,
that his son, a computer analyst,
can't find a job in Los Angeles.
Those eyes of a defeated novelist who
has lived in his dream too long
flicker back and forth; and when
he asks if we're Christians
  I turn, swinging on my pack
and hustle you up the trail.
Now always in the daylight before me
are your nalgitas, two golden apples
born from the night, the myth
almost substantial for the rest of the day,
the golden horse's tail of your hair.
He needs a friend you say,
but I don't believe a thing he says,
a theophany dogging us, singing around corners,
over boulders. I have a terrible vision
of sharing lunch with him. And so
just like an expert, at my low hiss,
a touch of the hand you dive
into the brittlebush and we lie flat
just off the trail, two animals
camouflaged in our own flesh
as he goes pounding up the path
of crushed rock full of himself. But in an hour
he astounds us, catching us
upright in the open, a ghost who's seen a ghost
rushing past chin out, muttering
            that he forgot to turn the water off in the bathroom.

Later, screened in the bushes
squinting at the ash-throated flycatcher
crazily alive, I decide there's nothing to do
                                        but live with the worst risks
we carry in our hearts. I impress you
imitating the cluckings of the crissal thrasher
with a shiny blade of grass, and in return
after thinking it over, you hold your nose,
make the sound of a horse drinking water—to do it again
that night at the party, announcing it a little
drunk, while after, delighted, everyone applauds
not knowing what else to do.

PAINTING THE MORMON CHURCH

When God looks down,
a balloon like the Michelin tire man
with freaky eyes, but instead of in a rush
                                        waving a bloated hand to us,
slowly floating over in great dispassionate bounds,
He likes to see things in order,
hedges trimmed, traffic moving
                        confidently through neighborhoods
knowing where it's going, as we did once
eyes beaming over the miniature village
neat beside our model railroad.
That's why I guess when I got up yesterday
the Mormons were out spending their day off
on bending ladders chipping paint,
calling to one another hauling buckets
of yellow paint up, while one sat
        off by himself on another part of the roof
legs splayed, gazing around beneath his baseball cap
as if on vacation, then turning back
to work threw a carrot stub down into the bushes.
Or why I got up today so early,
putting on my suit went jogging out past them
fists to chest as they streamed in,
nails cleaned by now and their women
                                        leading chains of children,
bearing their wonderfully huge and wild
breasts perfumed before them in their halters,
so rich they can feed armies of the blessed,
or why an hour later I came running back around the corner
just in time to see them streaming out again,
working off nervous energy, keeping
this desiccated body going, ridiculously
filling my lungs with quarts of air.

ROACH MOTELS

Coming undone again on Saturday night,
dancing for hours around the little adobe house, our joy
from the week unreeling from our heads, I yell
"Watch out for the critters in the bathroom,
the traps I've set for them, brown, intelligent
thumbs alert on the porcelain," when you go dancing in.
But you've bought these things before in the stores
you shout back, call, and I barge in to see it,
the plastic perfectly landscaped, like the scenery
that graces model trains, or what one sees
full of expectation flying low over a city just before landing,
the cars parked out front, the hedges with their shiny haircuts,
and here the roaches streaming between them
"to check in, but not out," according to the
advertisement you whisper,
                                        like businessmen anywhere
eager to get about their business, a nod
from the waitress, a good night's sleep, or to lie awake
in their socks thinking about how the day went.
The design's for us you say back through your falling
gold scallops, like dog biscuits in the shape of mailmen
about to get bit. But once you say,
daring me, you looked and inside there was wallpaper,
miniature chairs, and in the rooms,
some singly, but others with dozens of them
welded to their cups of coffee, the television sets
they first stooped to touch, or neckties off straining,
staring at the ceiling trying to think of a symphony,
of the day of the week as if their lives depended on it
and dying standing up because they can't.
I start to think of the frozen horse at Stalingrad,
                                                                        of normal Faustus
electrocuted upright by the wonders of mind and flesh,
then finding that they actually work, delighted,
lean over your long freckled body to pull down the shades,
shut the little plastic doors on that.

GRAMMAR SCHOOL

Raising hell in the playground
            our heads jangled when the bell rang,
for that prolonged moment inside the bell itself,
then ran in to sit in the light of the mullions,
        all afternoon reading aloud,
our mouths gaping around the precision
                    of Latin, Greek, the languages
that enriched our own, made us special.
Not knowing that they also had their ancients,
who believing in themselves taught their students.
with the light of their own classics, making
in the end diplomats, sub-pharaohs
of those who best wrote them down, who for years
peering into their faith copied the past
word for word on rabbit skins, and thus
taking their prized scrolls with them, their confidence,
were best equipped to rule a world.
                                        And when
such an honored man died
his friends took them out again, wound
the corpse in their layers,
            binding it around with the furry
power of his language to better
gird him, sealed in honey, into the next life.
And because they knew that men
                    can hear their friends
for a brief moment after they're dead, still
believing in themselves each took his turn,
            stepping up, leaning close, whispering
tenderly, "Don't forget. Don't forget,"

Doing the job so well
that stumbling on such a discovery
we don't dare unravel them
but spend years scanning
                those far-off continents
from the distances of our radioscopes,
they are that fragile, that powerful.

GOLD MINES

All day I've been up in the mountains
running in and out of the line, popping
up ahead to make jokes at them,
a congregation that so full of joy
with itself at last decided to leave its church,
strike out for the sea of pink lemonade
or whatever it was they were dreaming of for years,
but in our case simply to see some birds,
shout into old mine shafts, throw stones down them,
make a frolic through the hills and at the pass
calling enough, eat the lunches drawn from our packs,
compare our hands going through the air
like airplanes or the lettuce flapping
                                    between slices of bread to
the clouds going by us and out into the desert—
the place where I look up to hear Donald Duck squabbling,
later answered by Walter Cronkite with throat cancer,
one of us in a T-shirt, hands on hips
speaking to himself. "Check that one out,"
I nudge the leader, who looks,
                                                    who's seen him before,
a patient on parole from the clinic.
When we start back he stays behind,
a firedrake scowling down on us from a cliff.
Does he have a gun, will he heave boulders
                                                 in some impolite outburst?
But no, the shrinks know their work, and at last he falls
in at the end of the embarrassed line.
                                                            When we get home
there's still enough light and
after such an easy trip of it I put on
my jogging clothes, go huffing and puffing
around the neighborhood glad-handing friends
   up on their roofs, polishing cars,
                                    getting ready for the best of Saturday,
but not really in earnest, a dragonfly dragging its legs,
and not so much for more exercise as
to look down again, check my own breath
where my treasure is, but not follow it into the night.

PETE THE LAST TASTYKAKE HORSE

We all have stories we want to tell
as if they were important.
Not he, propelled for twenty years
by so much sweetness,
the man perched behind him with a whip,
a sentence
not spoken. Benevolently waiting
he watched him
arbitrarily going into houses
with his wicker basket holding
Easter eggs, gallstones
oozing something creamy, tipping his cap
to the housewife, driving to the next.
That life had everything to recommend it,
the tug of the blue-and-gold wagon,
and in spring the trees going by in their new confections,
once in a while rusted chickens flying out of them.
He knew his name, but never cared to speak it.
That was heaven. And at night
collected to the sanctum sanctorum of the stalls
drowsing with the others through the sunlight of it again,
disturbed only now and then
by rumors of retirement
when he'd be driven West
to run wild, fend for himself with his ancestors
beneath the Brazil nuts of the planets,
among Mona Lisas thrown down into the arborescent cactus,
from this hill and that the watery eyes
of camelopards poking up to watch him.
But eased
in the morning by the man who appeared first,
after a night of beating his wife
tugging his uniform straight, taking
a snort of whiskey, cooing to him,
stroking him back into shape.

GOLD

Halfway to Mowry and Lochiel,
the ghost towns hidden among these gramineous hills
    dotted with mesquite groves, almost landscaped,
we hear a gnashing in the truck's rusted bowels,
something in the solenoid, the chain-link drive
no doubt. What shall we do up here,
abandoned with just our sandwiches? Our minds
faint back over the dirt road to the last town
creeping across the desert away from itself, back
a hundred miles to a mechanic, a city, real civilization.
We park and because it's early and
                    we've come so far hike anyway,
in a couple of hours winding up a hill so high
we can see there, behind other hills, the shacks
tucked away, the abandoned hill towns where the grumpy miners
survive, delighted in the handful of gold
they work all year for, while their children
starve, become more idiotic, and their wives grouse
                              as they throw the dishwater out. At
the top sunstruck suck on our water bottles,
lounge about like tourists pointing to the smoke, the clouds
of a cold front boiling over a range far to the north.
By now the cows are bellowing below among the trees
stretching across a landscape of shadows moving over gold.
    When you put on your windbreaker,
your scarf, I love you even more. This is
a transcendental world I almost call out
from the top, turning and turning around for the views. And so
we head on down to our fate, to the truck
that starts, that bounces right on past
the grumpy towns, a couple hours on the freeway home,
healing itself, just as we believe things should do.

THE CONTINGENT

Done with their weeks of hunting
the Indians sit around grinning at one another
while their bulky wives chew the hides
into moccasins, spit into ollas to make wine.
Then one looking his fellows in the eye
makes his ribs ripple like the clappers in wind chimes;
one lights his pipe and turns a nearby mountain
into a volcano spouting entrails of wisdom, while a third,
a fourth, points up at the sky
                    become a Niagara sucking itself in
or sends a storm of voices, a symphony orchestra gone mad
to wreck the cabin of their old neighbor the trapper.
But enough. When they're done proving this or that
they're ready for real fun again
and ride off screaming through camp,
thespians fully possessed by their aspirations
running through a lieutenant governors' convention,
and just in time for the event, to see
themselves topping a ridge, sit there a moment in the pines
snorting through their noses looking down at
a carriage bobbing along the plains with its contingent.
When they attack it's all over as soon
as it happens, the slaughter of chickens who won't quit,
the soldiers' eyeballs bugging out as they
crouch behind their guns firing in extremis,
not able to believe that their education
has been just for this, while in alarm she,
that princess escaping from the Revolution,
                    half leaps out the window
despairing to the clouds, and throwing up her arms
as if her breasts, the best of Jell-O,
young cheeses aging in plastic bags, will
prove their worth by bearing her up to heaven,
but pulled down by her wooden feet as she ascends
already feeling the sexual perversions
through the night, the constant rasp, heated
calves' breath at her ears, and seeing waving,
there, above her, her red fingers, her dishpan hands.

NOURISHMENT

Wanting only to be left alone,
to escape perhaps once a year
the loving plagues: a job, wife, children,
you lock the car, wander for days, hands
in pockets, straps hanging from your pack
around the desert foothills where a hundred years ago
the miners blasted the land with fire hoses
                                        washing out gold,
then ran through the dawn and sunset of their lives,
but as if by intent always spiralling upward
as if higher, where the rocks shine
Godlike in the rare air, the universe
                    and the soul will coalesce.
Until far back in the high Sierra, all day
passing trees that stand but hardly grow
you come upon a trapper's cabin, nearly preserved,
just big enough to lie down in, wood
stoked under the bed to make the place
a furnace the dazed man walked and walked around in
coming back frozen from his rounds,
only to go out again in the morning. That was before
women came to the country, bringing curtains,
insisting on schools. Was that more or less
of what Jefferson planned for the nation?
That night beginning to be afraid again
checking your food, you decide to sleep a ways away
on a little knoll, where zipped to the chin
you watch the last of the sky, an army
rushing over the peaks that sway a moment
as it passes, until like him you do sleep
but dreaming of legendary Norman Clyde, kicked out of school
at Lone Pine for threatening his students with a shotgun
and thereafter wandered here lock-jawed,
taking in everything, but carrying his Greek and Roman texts
wherever he went for the day's final nourishment.

INTUITION

The first time they
wandered around fingering your letters,
fed the dog, stopped
to wonder at the old brass lock
shaped like a squatting hog they'd pulled easily
as a tooth from the rotted wood of the window
so that when you got home
even as you came up the walk
you knew something was wrong,
wondered who had lain for a moment
on the bed, whether to call the police
or a psychiatrist. But next time
you are out crossing flooded rivers
leaping with combs and knives, playing word games
at the missions, asking the overfed, staring
Papago children to stand up, match one column
with another. When they get "green bear"
or "I walked with refrigerators for shoes"
and they fall to the floor as if instantly struck,
dissolve there into laughter before
the solicitous nuns knowing that's not right,
they come with their larger, uneducated cousins
who break down the door with a crowbar,
back up a truck and take everything
so that days later when you come back
you find the cupboards open to the
breathless linoleum, the bed standing
in just its springs like an awkward naked woman,
and the retired farmacéutico in his
traditional suspenders, the landlord
with his wife and children gathered
across the street as if they have seen
a bad star, as if you have already
moved without saying good-bye.

FLORESCENCE

The palm grows so high
in order to lift its florescence,
a shining cluster of plastic kites.

On Saturday I see you
pausing on your walk already stunned,
a fisherman with a net tied around your head,
something gauzy looking around
                    just stepped out of the grave,

Watch you climb as awkward
as an astronaut, leave the ladder, disappear
into the waving tentacular heart up there.
What shoots out I think at first
is your head spurting sideways,
a cloud taking off to join the others
    jogging toward Mexico without a thought,

But then you come down,
a fireman on his slick pole
                    but hands flailing
at the fire on his face,
missing the last few steps.

Your arthritic wife runs out
to where you lie still kicking on the lawn
to coo over you all night as
the women did full of fear,
                    trying to comfort
Moses gone wild again, stuttering
about the vision he'd come down with.

REAL FORESTS

On Friday nights we are up on our toes playing darts,
while out back of the church
our little gruff dog is barking through the bushes
at the Mormons squaredancing in the alley,
                    coming together, breaking apart.
The more Carlo Rossi we drink
the more clothes we take off,
leaning forward past all our naked parts
toward the target.
They're trying to remember the long journey
across the continent, the slaughtered men,
the gold tablets, the babbling ravished women,
                and at the ends of their lives
when they remember perfectly, released,
will go shooting off toward their planets,
the wind in their teeth, to be hauled aboard
before they whizz past by all their welcoming relatives,
while we, having also labored,
                trying to forget the week,
will lie down somewhere on our frayed Turkish rug,
heads in our spongy armpits drift off,
frenzied mice at last escaping daylight into the immense land
beyond the hole in the baseboard,
but not before seeing the flash, the painting
of a forest by Cézanne we once saw wandering in a museum,
which struck us, forest creatures though we are,
                as much better than any real forest.

PHOTOGRAPHIC MEMORIES

Each day you go out before them,
a female epileptic possessed
as she shakes at the miracle, the new cactus ears,
green escaped from maps of the oceans,
pointing with such horror and delight that
erasers bubble from your mouth
as you whirl your blond horsetail
subscribed by your breasts
spinning out spirals of milk,
until overcome by the pleasure,
you fall down mumbling.
You're no farm girl;
I lead you in to a common breakfast,
pancakes, scrambled eggs laid out all in order,
talk about the stock report.
But new to nature, you want to say
they are clocks keeping their own time through the seasons,
the frontiersmen you read about who sleep all winter
dreaming of running out, becoming fat on buffalo,
or the child who in an early stage
has photographic memory,
and after years of troubling his parents
makes one grand painting
before he quits to become an adult.
Always remembering the orderly slaughter
that kept us alive on the farm,
I keep you in balance with kisses,
bites on the lip, and at night
walk you hand in hand to the corner market
to buy the favors you pick, stuff you
with the continuing cure, ice cream, doughnuts,
to walk back home, the flavors of it,
pictures still glowing in the cave of your mouth;
the moment we stand in the door of the hot house,
all the clocks begin rocking on tiptoes,
ringing with ideas
above the encyclopedias fallen from the shelf,
writhing on the floor as they speed through their pages.

PICKING UP NAILS

Cross at the workmen who come to work
in a frenzy for their wages, only
to leave for days to get drunk
or whatever they do, I graze
around the tomb of the new room
among the broken timbers they threw from the roof,
the bricks jumbled on pallets, the lumps of concrete
scattered around, as if instead
of going up, something were coming down. And tortured by
the vision of it, the nights with a bottle of Bolla
and a girl around the blazing beehive fireplace,
days screwed to the desk, snowed in,
waiting for something warm to come out,
holding my can, an old tin of Sir Walter Raleigh
I saved, pick up nails. Just
    then I remember my great-uncle,
who never married but lived barefoot in a wooden cottage
so rustically he watched the bricks fall off his chimney
                                        one by one over the years,
the wind blow right through the slats of the house,
and decorated the inside with his own paintings of Christ
rising like smoke from the local factories,
so penurious he saved the snippings
from his grapes, bound them with twine
into the neat bundles that kept him warm at night,
but so thoughtful he left a whole cellarful
of wine to the church. For decades
people marveled at communion over the taste
of it growing better and better as they
remembered him less and less. And so
we have those other, perhaps more lavish explorers,
who traveling widely enriched history,
                              kneeling alone in their canoes
to hear the fishes cry, or to flatter queens
sped across oceans to establish colonies,
so confident they dared to marry Indian princesses.

PRIVATE LIVES

With the last of my money
I have bought you a garden,
its background strawberry sherbet
so overlaid by a delicate grillwork, a rusted arabesque
of ovaries, gears, and connecting plum vines,
such as the Swiss psychiatrist saw in his original dream,
the best one he ever had,
that it would break of its own weight
        if lifted out, struck full by the sunlight.
Such as Thomas Jefferson pondered sucking on his hookah
at Monticello studying the layout of the Palace of Versailles
trying to discover the essence of French bread.
Nailed to the wall above the bed
it floats away, an exquisite postage stamp,
the prize drifting from the collector who
strains and strains after it trying to recognize
something he remembers, at least thinking
he hears music. Nevertheless when we
simply step, two cotyledons out of our clothes
and go to bed we sleep arms bent
over our heads, the best sleep we've ever had
as it comes back, plays for us nearly
all night as if the sheikh, tired of his long art,
of the delight in his crimes, ordered out the band
one Sunday afternoon, the bandsmen
sent away for years to be trained by the British,
dressed like the British, just for this,
and happy to blare their horns back into the sunlight,
happier still at the prospect, a job well done,
walking home to call out to their wives. But not
as he did building the estate all his life
toward the idea of it always in his head,
                                the years knocking out walls,
rearranging flower beds that never quite fit, going
deeper and deeper into the debt of his private life.

FARMER

Two or three times a year
the farmer goes to town
leaving his wife behind him gawking in the door.
But he doesn't have to worry
as he drives through the hardwood forests of the Catskills
past the storytelling maples, the tulip trees
        putting out buds that later frenzied musicians from Hungary
    will make into pianos, play
                like captive women in New York.
Behind him are the blocks of butter
        bearing his own acorn stamp, gold on its way to the bank
    kept cool by swaths of crabgrass,
            blue ink under water, that through all the bouncing
        creep back and forth over them,
so that when the Indians leap up
        full of passion, teeth bared from ambush,
    seeing it they sink back instantly converted for the moment,
        lie there on the oak leaves in their swaddling clothes
            blitzed, dreaming of their myths.

So that days later when he comes back
        there's a smile on his face,
    he goes directly to his cows
        to feed them the apple turnovers he's brought
        that they look at like storybooks,
            the éclairs that explode past their faces,
            souls whizzing straight to heaven when they open them,
        their treasury of merits,
and hearing it his wife comes stumbling out
    tripping on the columbine, her long skirts,
    horrified within herself behind her flayed hands
        from all those days of washing dishpans, his underpants.

PIANO PLAYER

Each morning when I manage to get up early,
like the monks did getting a jump on their salvation
by praying, singing anthems for hours,
an assembly of men out of respect for God, Who is Holiness,
only moving their lips, then taking that joy within
with them, handwarmers, censers working all day in the fields,

Still osmatic, not completely whole
I stumble in my shorts from window to window,
to be sure the neighbors are still asleep,
kings still in their rich jails, that
the bulbous car out front is still comatose,
like the silverware on the drain board not having
                    started itself up, become excited
with ideas of foreign travel.

That takes a while, checking everything out,
as difficult as the concerned young doctor curing chlorosis,
trying not to fall in love with the girl because
he knows her parents trust him. Actually
there's no stopping it, and by the time
I've made my twelfth or thirteenth round
here comes the sun, daytime ghost having fun
throwing off his robes, his onion eye
peeling and peeling off opalescent rings of fire
as it peeks up over the Santa Catalina Mountains.

And in that first light inspired or frightened I rush in
to see you suffrutescent, lying there
summa cum laude in the sheets among your blond hair
as on tiptoes the little dog runs along paws stretched up
on the edge of the bed, a pianist, hair slicked back,
playing a huge piano, a picaroon in tails trying
to outdistance his desire speeding back and forth
eating a great ear of corn as one sees sometimes
in the comic strips. One eye opens
and though panting he listens for a moment,
then begins playing your requests, *The Moonlight Sonata*,
something from *The Sound of Music*, a bit rushed
                              perhaps but as fresh, as beautiful
as their composers first heard them
                              before writing them down.

TIMBER THIEVES

The things that God gives to the world
are the excrescences of the earth,
the gold knobs shining on the hills
and the water that leaps out of rocks, looks around
to become the venous rivers braiding the valleys.
And so the trees, the Douglas fir and the balsam,
they are the confident hands of God, permanent treasures
to the nations, who sit back, preserve them
like feathers in a cap,
except there are always those,
cogeners of their drunken fathers
who put decals on the windows of their trucks,
who shoot dogs and carry them, the disgraced host
stricken through the streets on their backs.
Forgetting their cousins growing thin
as gruel toward their spirits in jail,
they revel in bars, and leaving by the back doors
sneak into the forest, wrenches big as leg bones
thrown over their shoulders.
Behind their gloved hands blown up
like balloons they pull out
the supple spruces, a black walnut
worth a thousand dollars or more
with the joy of strangling a sister,
take them home, feed them to the cows,
build a boat, the fastest thing on the water,
or unable to contain themselves
call their brothers-in-law on the phone
who come over in a moment with all their tools,
working a few hours present them
with a new dining-room table to support flowers
for their wives, a cabinet for their records.
And so they sit, immune postulants dressed
in their fringed cowboy clothes, soft kangaroo boots,
comfortable all night, for the rest of their lives
before the wood that like a jukebox, an aurora borealis
flashes with the sad continuous stories of the disciples.

MOUNTAIN LION

Lieutenant of the guard,
he grows weary though young
of standing outside the castle
all night in a uniform as handsome
                                        as a greeting card
while the great soft snow, mocking
popcorn, falls around him,
Gresham's law coming apart. Before him
is the woods that goes on and on toward France
with its C students, wolves
        howling through the tangle after their muscae volitantes,
while off to the right in a cove the village
lies, a lost pocketbook closed up
with a few holes burning raggedly through.
He strains with his afterbrain for the sounds within,
a tune clunking backwards through a music box,
the favored swains making up songs, breaking
furniture stumbling through their apartments,
while the king, a burlap bag of charcoal
coming to life, pursues the queen again,
who richly indignant at last gives up.
For this reason, feeling the insult
to his own education, he lays down his gun,
walks off, starts to run through a lifetime
that takes in whole mountain ranges
as his sole domain, snapping up rabbits
as he goes, gashing out bark and lumps of wood,
to lie still some afternoons on a ledge
                                in the midst of his new musculature,
always alone, his own ghostly presence,
already become a French painter, his own ornate chaise longue,
while back at the castle in the morning
they stumble out, discover the blots of his tracks
bounding off. That's the blast of cold air
that sobers up drunken men,
who come to their senses, pursue the monster.

WASHING WINDOWS

All day we make our clockwise circle around the house,
you on the inside, me on the out,
going through the motions, the awkward ballet
                    of some purgatorial experiment,

Our polishings the matched waves,
                    one pressed against the other,
nodding, tapping, rubbing out this streak and that.
What is that you're saying? Mine or yours?

I shout trying to remember what I did at the party last night.
Did you really do your kickup dance from the *West Side Story*
and did I, late, whirl around with a lamp shade on my head,
arms out in hilarious mockery of the cliché and myself?

Nevertheless finally it's done, and having spent
just a few hours from our lives we're back
to where we started, grinning at one another, at our prospect:

To sit inside for one moment of the year purged at last,
completely sober, watching the wind outside,
that vagrant never so transparent staggering around the neighborhood.

MILO

There you go again in the winter
sun that staggers over all day
casting milo among the mesquite and cactus,
out around the slumping adobe garage
where your paintings fill the racks,
sunsets that look like bears sliding down claws raised,
or deserts that might be the miniature scenes
grim Indians make of cactus candy under plastic
and sell to tourists at Stuckey's.
                                        We've said it before,
and all it takes as I reach through
the railroad-tie fence to pat frantic Lulu on the head,
throw her iridescent tennis ball as she pants—
as you stop in mid swing—is a wink:
you sow birdseed only to reap birdshit.
Though I see you later that afternoon out back
covered with paint among the thin fountaining creosote,
your fortune floating down around you at last,
                    lighting on your shoulders, arms, your hands,
threshing as if they might bear you away.

COCKERPOOS

They weren't looking for themselves at all,
the dogs that bore them through lost childhoods
or where to clear a sunny spot in that jungle, plant
the roots, stubs of fine cigars itching in their pockets
to produce a purer grape juice to please the king back home.
Any other way they knew of cheering as they knelt
beneath a symbol cut their fingers with their two-edged swords:
all they wanted was gold, like carrot juice, a rare
kind of vitamin for their souls.
And so what did they do having lost
their shoes, their ragged clothes, and beyond help
like minds cut loose at last coming
to the stone house and peering in saw
the fuzzy cockerpoos floating past the windows
in a kind of limbo, marking time
in the limited ecstasy of their own pursuit.
                                        Like rubber hoses
their swords bounced off the door.
And prowling around out back found
the women growing from poles in the untended garden
in pods larger than the largest cucumbers, which
broke open, sleeping corpses come to life again,
each a dawn stepping out of a body bag
    in her nightclothes at their approach.
What to do? The simplemindedness they stepped into reigned
all around crowned in the marriages with these ammoniacal women,
as they slept together, paid their bills among the scriptures of wilder
  fruits.
And now remembering dimly, their tularemic children
stand on street corners blowing their plastic horns
or whirl off like the just converted sowing the wind
with the pages of comic books they tear out.
While above in those ancient tamarisks
        brought from Europe the doctors in their white coats
look off long-eared at the daytime stars through their stethoscopes,
while others nod, hands in pockets, bark low to one another.

WHALES

Though they howl all day
at the sun and moon out of shape,
after they're startled for long the animals become docile,
and so they come in defeated couples
noses scanning the ground and up the ramp
into this strange place where the drunken man shouts
and behind him his wife complains,
to be borne off like this in their closet
full of relatives and the earth's wealth.
Only the fish remain, feeling a rising,
a slow explosion all around them, to survive
though at first confused wandering in their own element.
Some get together, want to build nests in trees,
in abandoned houses after the wistful corpses float out
for now they are indeed the earth's rightful birds,
pioneers with a huge inheritance,
while others who have always been wise
now realize it, and instead dive deep down,
on the bottom following the lights in their heads
graze on the lumps of scrannel coal
always waiting there glowing, as rich as uranium,
and like Shakers or the Pennsylvania Dutch
decide to establish their kingdom, lead a simple life,
building pine schoolhouses among the dunes
where together they rejoice, practice their singing.
Still every once in a while full of good fun,
for diversion
they take the journey, the long flight
chuckling all the way back up to the top.
That's what the whalers hear at night
lost in the weak light of their hollow ships,
sitting among their white locks,
hollow-eyed, still harried by women,
the slapping against the planks, the far-off coughs,
the laughter, the a cappella voices coming and going.

WEDDING

For one day man and wife
are king and queen of creation.
That's why they wear a crown, a paper tiara,
                    vestments embroidered with passementerie
as the village gathers around them in the town square.
His head is a nugget, hers a transcendent
        lump of mashed potatoes with parsley in it.

While they play the songs born from tradition,
                the best music anyone's ever heard,
he theorematic dreams of becoming a mathematician,
she of lying down on one elbow, bearing children
who with their strong buttery spirits will save
the town from floods by inventing new grapevines.

With this on their minds, they set off toward their new home,
toward their chamber secretly decorated
                                with boughs, oak parquetry
to find the first love that their lives
                        thereafter will be built on,
but being farmers first check the new barn
where the zebras poised for hours begin to play their basses,
those always frightened pilots the chickens
                    follow their scales up to the loft
and the heavy cows being full, embarrassed, low
as best they can the moment he throws the door open.